JOSEPH – LIFE IS A PARADOX

A STORY OF BETRAYAL, FORGIVENESS & FULFILMENT

Lessons from a Therapist's Perspective

Oforiwah Penney-Laryea

Dedication

To my amazing children, Enoch, Luan, and Mapenzi, I love you so much. Also, to all the young people who have dreams in their hearts to fulfill, it is possible to go through a challenging process patiently and honorably. Work hard and trust in God, who is faithful to help you fulfill it.

Acknowledgments

To my friend, Mrs. Margaret Takyi-Micah, thank you for reading my first draft of this book and providing me with honest feedback. I truly appreciate your time and effort.

To my family, my husband, Enoch Penney-Laryea, and our children, Enoch, Luan, and Mapenzi, you are my number one cheerleaders. Your support and prayers mean the world to me, and I am immensely grateful for your love. Thank you all for reading this book and offering your valuable and encouraging feedback.

I am grateful to Sasha F. for the beautiful illustration on the book's cover.

Many thanks to my editor Celest A. for a great job done and also for the positive feedback.

Finally, I thank God Almighty for granting me the grace to write this book and its story, which serves as a great inspiration to me. I am also thankful for providing me with all the resources and direction I needed. May His name be praised!

Contents

Dedication ii

Acknowledgments iii

Contents iv

Prologue vi

Introduction vii

CHAPTER 1 1
Joseph's Dreams & Betrayal 1

CHAPTER 2 10
In Potiphar's House 10

CHAPTER 3 13
Prison 13

CHAPTER 4 17
In The Presence Of Pharaoh 17

CHAPTER 5 27
Fulfillment 27

CHAPTER 6 33
Tears of Joy 33

CHAPTER 7 38
The Test 38

CHAPTER 8 42
Forgiveness 42

CHAPTER 9 51
Reunion 51

CHAPTER 10 54

Final Words of Jacob   **54**

CHAPTER 11   **57**
Family Tree of Jacob   **57**

CHAPTER 12   **59**
God's Good Plans   **59**

CHAPTER 13   **62**
Life Is a Paradox   **62**

References   **65**

Prologue

"As for you, you meant evil against me, but God meant it for good, to bring it about that many people should be kept alive, as they are today" (Genesis 50:20, English Standard Version).

Introduction

The purpose of this book is to encourage the reader, using the life story of Joseph in the Bible, not to give up on your dream no matter how insurmountable your challenges may be. Be patient, work, and persevere through the difficulties until you finally realize your dream.

"For the vision is yet for an appointed time, but at the end, it will speak and it will not lie: though it tarries, wait for it because it will surely come, it will not tarry" (Habakkuk 2:3, New King James Version).

Every difficult or challenging situation provides an opportunity for one to learn and improve one's character. In other words, growth in character occurs through patience and perseverance in life's troubles.

The story of Joseph shows that there are no shortcuts in life. Trying to shorten the process of what you are going through by opting for the cheaper and easier route will deprive you of the lessons to learn and the character to build in order to live your dream. Additionally, it's important to forgive those who betray or wrong you in order to have a free heart that will propel you to achieve your dream. Not forgiving others is a distraction and will strangle your dream.

Joseph's life draws our attention to the faithfulness of God throughout the unbelievably difficult times of betrayal, serving an unjustifiable prison sentence, and pursuing his dream career.

Most importantly, the Joseph story teaches us that in all things, you should "trust in the Lord with all your heart and lean not on your own understanding. In all your ways acknowledge Him, and He shall direct your paths" (Proverbs 3:5-6, New King James Version).

Chapter 1

Joseph's Dreams & Betrayal

Joseph was a good-looking seventeen-year-old boy who lived with his family in Canaan, which later became known as Israel. Joseph's father, Jacob, was also called Israel. His mother, Rachel, died in the process of giving birth to Benjamin, Joseph's younger brother. Rachel had a difficult labor and did not survive after the delivery of her baby.

Joseph had eleven brothers and one sister, but only Benjamin shared the same mother and father as Joseph. His half-brothers included Reuben, Simeon, Levi, Judah, Issachar, and Zebulun, and he had one sister named Dinah, whose mother was Leah. His other brothers, Dan and Naphtali, had Bilhah as their mother, while Zilpah gave birth to Gad and Asher, his other siblings. Reuben was Jacob's firstborn child and therefore, the eldest among all the siblings.

Jacob married Leah and Rachel, who were sisters. This came about because Jacob fell in love with Rachel and decided to marry her. However, Laban, Rachel's father, tricked him into marrying Leah, the older sister, first because, according to Laban, this was their custom. In Laban's defense, he said that customarily, the younger sister could not marry until the older sister had married. Therefore, after marrying Leah, Jacob had to pursue the love of his life and marry Rachel as his second wife.

Jacob loved Joseph more than all of his children because he had Joseph when he was old. As a result, Jacob made him a coat of many colors. It became evident to Joseph's brothers that their father loved Joseph more than all of them, leading to sibling rivalry. Consequently, they all hated Joseph and could not have peaceful conversations with him.

One day, Joseph had a dream, and when he narrated it to his brothers, it increased their hatred for him. Joseph told his brothers, "Hear this dream that I have dreamed: Behold, we were binding sheaves in the field, and my sheaf arose and stood upright. And behold your sheaves gathered around it and bowed down to my sheaf" (Genesis 37:6-7 English Standard Version). So his brothers asked him if he would indeed rule over them. This dream further fueled Joseph's brothers' hatred for him.

Then, on another occasion, Joseph had another dream which he told his brothers and said, "Behold, I have dreamed another dream. Behold the sun, the moon, and eleven stars were bowing down to me" (Genesis 37:9). However when Joseph narrated this to his father and brothers, his father scolded him and said, "What is this dream that you have dreamed? Shall I and your mother and your brothers indeed bow ourselves to the ground before you?" (Genesis 37:10). While this second dream made Joseph's brothers resent him even more, his father kept it in his mind.

Jacob was a shepherd, and as was their practice, his sons would usually send the flock miles away to graze in the deep fields. On this particular occasion, Joseph's brothers sent the flock to graze in Shechem. While his brothers were away, Jacob, perhaps growing concerned, sent Joseph to check on his brothers and the flock to ensure everything was okay. When Joseph reached Shechem, he made inquiries and was told that his brothers had left for Dothan, where he finally found them. As Joseph approached his brothers from a distance, they plotted to kill him and concoct a lie that a beast had eaten him up. This was their way of putting an end to Joseph and his annoying dreams. However, Reuben, their eldest brother, advised against killing Joseph, suggesting instead that they throw him into an empty pit nearby. Reuben intended to rescue Joseph and send him home after his brothers had left.

Upon Joseph's arrival, his brothers stripped him of his beautiful coat of many colors and threw him into an empty, dry pit. As the brothers sat down to eat, they noticed a group of Ishmaelite traders coming from Gilead with their camels carrying myrrh, balm, and other spices. These traders were headed to Egypt. At this point, Judah convinced his brothers to sell Joseph instead of killing him because, after all, he was their own brother. They heeded Judah's advice and sold Joseph to the Ishmaelite traders for twenty shekels of silver. These traders continued their journey and took Joseph to Egypt.

Reuben, who was absent when his brothers sold Joseph, returned to the pit only to find it empty. Obviously, his brothers had kept secret what they had done to Joseph. Reuben was frantic and returned to his brothers, not knowing what to do. That was when they agreed to kill a goat and dip Joseph's coat in its blood to perpetuate their lies and narrative. Upon reaching home, the brothers showed the bloodied coat to their father, Jacob, who immediately recognized it as Joseph's. Jacob then concluded that a beast had killed and eaten Joseph. He tore his clothes and put on sackcloth, as was their custom for mourning. Jacob genuinely believed that his son Joseph had died due to the evidence of his robe covered in blood. He wept bitterly and mourned his son for many days, refusing to be comforted by his other children because of his overwhelming grief.

Lessons

1. Sibling rivalry is the competition and jealousy among siblings. Although sibling rivalry is common in families with two or more children, the way parents treat their children affects the bond between them. Some important factors that affect sibling relationships are the order in which children are born and the treatment each child receives from their parents. In this case, Joseph was born to Jacob in his old age, which gave him a special place in his father's heart. This special treatment included the gift of a coat of many colors. Sibling rivalry is reduced when parents make efforts to give each child the attention needed, create an environment for siblings to have fun together, and avoid favoritism.

2. It is not prudent to communicate one's dreams hastily, especially if the person involved does not have your best interests at heart. When God gives you a dream, or you have a dream, you must protect and nurture it. At the right time, as you feel led, you could reveal the dream to the right person or persons whom you absolutely trust. Joseph could have shared his dreams with his father, not his siblings, because they were jealous of him and would not engage in peaceful conversations with him.

3. Joseph was betrayed by his own brothers, who betrayed his love for them and his trust in them by intentionally hurting him deeply through the following actions:

   a. Initially, Joseph's brothers decided to kill him out of jealousy and a desire to put an end to his annoying dreams. However, their oldest brother, Reuben, advised against killing Joseph because he was their sibling. Instead, Reuben suggested throwing Joseph into an empty pit to rescue him later and send him back to their father.

   b. Joseph's brothers followed Reuben's advice, stripped him of his coat of many colors, and cast him into a dry, empty pit. Consequently, Joseph found himself naked and alone in the pit, exposed to the elements, likely weeping and starving, far away from home in Dothan.

   c. Furthermore, Joseph's brothers betrayed him by selling him to Ishmaelite traders for twenty shekels of silver.

The betrayal of Joseph by his brothers must have come as a complete shock to him, leaving him confused, lonely and sad, just to name a few of the hurtful emotions associated with betrayal by a loved one. It must have also been a very traumatic experience for Joseph because of all the above suffering his brothers put him through.

Some Helpful Tips to Help You Deal with Betrayal

a. Normally, one is betrayed not because of anything they have done wrong, but because of their betrayer's own selfish needs, just as in the case of Joseph. Joseph's brothers were jealous of him and wanted to get rid of him due to his dreams that indicated he would become ruler over them in the future. Also, Judas Iscariot betrayed Jesus Christ not because of anything Jesus did wrong but because of Judas's own selfish needs and love for money (Luke 22:1-6, 47-54).

b. It is helpful to be able to know and name how you are feeling. For example, if you feel sad, confused, angry, or lonely. This will help you work through the betrayal and move past it with time.

c. There is a tendency to want to get revenge when you have been betrayed. However, try to refrain from that because revenge will hurt you more and prolong your hurt. It will help you if you focus on yourself and forgive your betrayer. This will enable you to move on in life and pursue your dreams and other future relationships.

d. Examine your relationship with this person who betrayed you.

   i. Is this person a close family member, a very good friend, or somebody quite distant?

ii. Is this the first time this person has betrayed you, or has it happened before?

iii. What kind of betrayal was it? Is it deliberate or not? For example, a deliberate betrayal is normally premeditated, where the betrayer intentionally hurts you, like in Joseph's case, or in your marriage, at your workplace, or in your school. A non-deliberate betrayal is when the betrayer does something against you unintentionally, for example, provides information about you through a slip of the tongue, which is later used by others against you.

Examining all of these aspects of the relationship with your betrayer would help you decide your relationship with him or her going forward.

e. Furthermore, suppose you find it difficult to work through the betrayal by yourself. In that case, it is important to talk to somebody you trust or a professional therapist or counselor who can help you deal with and heal from the betrayal so that you can move on in life. It might take some time, but you will be able to work through it with help.

4. Sometimes, the experiences we encounter may look, without a shadow of a doubt, as though they are the truth, but in reality, it might be a "mirage," as was the

case of Joseph's purported death. If Jacob had harmed himself because of the fictitious death of Joseph, it would have been a very sad story, as we would later see in this book. On the other hand, the dream wouldn't have been realized if Joseph had harmed himself through the betrayal and trauma. So, have patience and keep hope alive to achieve the dream.

Chapter 2

In Potiphar's House

Joseph was brought to Egypt by the Ishmaelite traders who bought him. Upon arrival, Joseph was purchased by an Egyptian named Potiphar, who served as an officer of Pharaoh and captain of the guard. Potiphar was impressed by Joseph's intelligence and noticed that God was with him, causing everything Joseph did to prosper. As a result, Joseph found favor with his master and was appointed as the head supervisor over Potiphar's household and all his possessions. After Joseph's promotion, God continued to bless everything owned by Potiphar, both at home and in the fields. Consequently, Potiphar was able to relax and had no concerns, with Joseph taking charge of the household, leaving Potiphar only to move to the dining table for meals.

Joseph was a handsome young man, and over time, his master's wife developed a strong desire for him. She persistently tried to engage in an amorous relationship with him. However, Joseph consistently refused her advances, stating that he could not repay his good master with such wickedness and that he could not sin against God.

So one day, when Joseph went into the house to work, none of the men who worked there were around. That was when his master's wife grabbed Joseph by his clothes, saying, "Lie with me" (Genesis 39:7). But Joseph left his clothes in her hands, took to his heels, and ran out of the house. She then called out to the men of the household and narrated the story to implicate Joseph as the one who wanted to force himself on her but ran away when she called for help.

When Potiphar came home, his wife told him the same story that she had told the men of the household and said, "The Hebrew servant whom you have brought among us came in to me to laugh at me. But as soon as I lifted up my voice and cried, he left his garment beside me and fled out of the house" (Genesis 39:17-18). As soon as Potiphar heard these words from his wife, he was enraged and therefore put Joseph in prison at the place where the king's prisoners were kept.

Nevertheless, God was with Joseph, showed him steadfast love, and favored him before the prison guard. The prison guard made Joseph a supervisor of all the prisoners in the prison and was responsible for everything that was done in there. The prison guard trusted in Joseph's capabilities and left everything in his care because God was with Joseph and made him successful in everything he did.

Lessons

1. Although Joseph was sold by his own brothers into slavery for doing nothing wrong, he was not an angry and bitter person. That is why he worked hard and did his best in managing his master's house, and God was with Joseph. Because of his positive attitude, God prospered Joseph, and he was successful in Potiphar's house, which led to his promotion by Potiphar to become the head supervisor of his house and everything he had.

2. Joseph was loyal to Potiphar his master and also revered God, which is why he decided in his heart not to have a sexual relationship with Potiphar's wife, despite her persistence to do so. As we can see from the story, Joseph's good character landed him in prison. Yes! Sometimes when you insist on doing the right thing, you end up in trouble or in conflict with some established norms. But guess what? Because he decided to do the right thing, God's presence continued to be with him, and even in prison, he was successful and was made supervisor of all the prisoners by the prison guard.

Chapter 3

Prison

While Joseph was in prison, two men joined him there who were King Pharaoh's cup-bearer and chief baker. These two guys committed an offense against Pharaoh, and that was why they were put in custody at the prison where Joseph was confined.

One night, both the cup-bearer and the baker had a dream, and the next morning, Joseph saw that both of them looked disturbed. Joseph inquired of Pharaoh's officers what was bothering them, and they told Joseph that they each had a dream and there was no one to interpret them. Then Joseph said to them, "Do not interpretations belong to God? Please tell them to me." (Genesis 40:8b). So the chief cup-bearer narrated his dream to Joseph as follows. He said in his dream, there was a vine before him which had three branches. Immediately, it budded, the flowers sprang up, and the clusters of grapes ripened. Then he saw Pharaoh's cup in his hand, in which he pressed the grapes and served it to Pharaoh. After hearing the dream, Joseph interpreted that in three days, Pharaoh would release him from prison and restore him to his office as the cup-bearer, where he would serve Pharaoh again. Joseph then pleaded with the chief cup-bearer to remember him after he had been restored to his former position with Pharaoh and ask Pharaoh to release him from prison because he did nothing wrong to be there.

The chief baker also narrated his dream to Joseph after listening to the interpretation of his colleague's dream. He said in his dream, he had three baskets on his head. In the topmost basket were different kinds of baked food, but birds were eating out of the basket on his head. Upon hearing the dream, Joseph interpreted that in three days, Pharaoh would release the chief baker from prison and hang him on a tree where birds would eat his flesh off his body.

On the third day after Joseph's interpretation of the dreams, it was Pharaoh's birthday. Pharaoh celebrated by organizing a feast for all his servants, and that was when he released both his chief cup-bearer and chief baker from prison. Pharaoh restored his chief cup-bearer to his former position, but he hanged his chief baker just as Joseph had interpreted to them.

Lessons

1. Joseph was a godly man and knew that the God he serves is omniscient. Joseph definitely had an encounter with his God; therefore, when

Pharaoh's officers had dreams and were worried because there was no one to interpret them, Joseph assured them that the interpretation of dreams comes from God. I believe that Joseph sought the face of God through prayer, and then God revealed the meaning of the dream to him. Joseph trusted in God and received the meaning of the dreams, which he told them. Accordingly, Joseph's interpretation of their dreams materialized. Joseph's heart was to help Pharaoh's officers by interpreting their dreams, but eventually, it was this gesture that would land him before Pharaoh and open the door to the fulfillment of his dreams and purpose in life. In difficult times, continue to trust in the faithfulness of God and do good.

2. Joseph asked for help. He told Pharaoh's cup-bearer that he should remember him after he had been released and restored back to his position with Pharaoh. Specifically, Joseph asked that he should tell Pharaoh the king to release him from prison because he had done nothing wrong. However, the chief cup-bearer forgot about Joseph and his request and did not remember him until what I would say was the right or appointed time. It is good to ask for help when you need it from the right person or people, just as Joseph

did. Asking for help is a sign of humility and an attitude to open up oneself to grace and mercy.

Chapter 4

In The Presence Of Pharaoh

Two years after Pharaoh had released his cup-bearer from prison and restored him back to his position, he had two dreams that troubled his spirit in the sense that it was concerning and disturbed him. In the first dream, Pharaoh stood by the river Nile and saw seven attractive fat cows that came out of the Nile and started to eat grass in the surrounding area. Just then, seven other cows that were ugly and lean also came out of the Nile and ate the seven attractive fat cows. Pharaoh woke up and fell asleep and had another dream. In the second dream, Pharaoh saw seven ears of grain that looked good and fat growing on a stalk. After this, he saw another seven ears of grain sprout, and this time they looked thin and damaged by the east wind. Then the seven thin ears of grain swallowed the seven fat ears of grain. When Pharaoh woke up the following morning, he was worried because of the dreams, so he assembled all the magicians and wise men of Egypt to interpret his dreams, but none of them could interpret them.

It was at this time that Pharaoh's chief cup-bearer remembered Joseph and how his interpretation of their dreams actually happened. So the chief cup-bearer said the following to Pharaoh, "I remember my offenses today. When Pharaoh was angry with his servants and put me and the chief baker in custody in the house of the captain of the guard, we dreamed on the same night, he and I, each having a dream with its own interpretation. A young Hebrew was there with us, a servant of the captain of the guard. When we told him, he interpreted our dreams to us, giving an interpretation to each man according to his dream. And as he interpreted to us, so it came about. I was restored to my office, and the baker was hanged." (Genesis 41:9-13).

When Pharaoh heard what his cup-bearer had narrated, he immediately sent for Joseph from the prison. Before Joseph came to see Pharaoh, he shaved himself and changed his clothes.

When Joseph arrived, Pharaoh told him that he had had dreams, but no one had been able to interpret them and that he had heard that Joseph is able to interpret dreams. Joseph responded that he is not the one who interprets the dreams but God.

After Pharaoh had recounted his dreams to Joseph, Joseph interpreted the dreams as follows, "The dreams of Pharaoh are one; God has revealed to Pharaoh what he is about to do. The seven good cows are seven years, and the seven good ears are seven years; the dreams are one. The seven lean and ugly cows that came up after them are seven years, and the seven empty ears blighted by the east wind are also seven years of famine. It is as I told Pharaoh; God has shown to Pharaoh what he is about to do. There will come seven years of great plenty throughout all the land of Egypt, but after them there will arise seven years of famine, and all the plenty will be forgotten in the land of Egypt. The famine will consume the land, and the plenty will be unknown in the land by reason of the famine that will follow, for it will be very severe. And the doubling of Pharaoh's dream means that the thing is fixed by God, and God will shortly bring it about. Now, therefore, let Pharaoh select a discerning and wise man, and set him over the land of Egypt. Let Pharaoh proceed to appoint overseers over the land and take one-fifth of the produce of the land of Egypt during the seven plentiful years. And let them gather all the food of these good years that are coming and store up grain under the authority of Pharaoh for food in the cities, and let them keep it. That food shall be a reserve for the land against the seven years of famine that are to occur in the land of Egypt so that the land may not perish through the famine." (Genesis 41:25-36).

Joseph's interpretation of Pharaoh's dreams and the proposal he made pleased Pharaoh and all of his servants. Then Pharaoh said to his servants, "Can we find a man like this, in whom is the Spirit of God?" (Genesis 41:38). So Pharaoh said to Joseph, "Since God has shown you all this, there is none so discerning and wise as you are. You shall be over my house, and all my people shall order themselves as you command. Only as regards the throne will I be greater than you. Pharaoh also said to Joseph, "See, I have set you over all the land of Egypt." Then Pharaoh took his ring from his finger and put it on Joseph's finger, dressed him in garments of fine linen, and put a gold chain around his neck. Additionally, Pharaoh made Joseph ride in his second chariot while his people called out before him saying, "Bow the knee!" (Genesis 41:39-43). That is how Pharaoh made Joseph ruler over the entire land of Egypt.

Pharaoh gave Joseph the name Zaphenath-paneah and a wife called Asenath, who was the daughter of Potiphera, priest of On. Joseph was thirty years old when he encountered Pharaoh King of Egypt and started serving him as second in command or Prime minister in Egypt. During the seven years when the earth produced food in abundance, Joseph gathered up all the food of the seven years in Egypt and stored it in all the cities. Joseph stored up grain in huge quantities such that he could not even measure them anymore.

During these years of abundance of food in Egypt, Joseph and Asenath, his wife had two sons. Joseph named their firstborn Manasseh for he said, "God has made me forget all my hardship and all my father's house" (Genesis 41:51). And he called their second son Ephraim, meaning, "For God has made me fruitful in the land of my affliction" (Genesis 41:52).

The seven years of abundance that happened in Egypt came to an end, and the seven years of famine began. There was famine everywhere; however, there was food in the entire land of Egypt. After a while, the people of Egypt started to experience severe hunger, and they cried to Pharaoh for food. Then, Pharaoh told the Egyptians to go to Joseph and do whatever he asked them to do. As a result of the severity of the famine, Joseph opened all the storehouses in Egypt and sold grain to the people. Also, because there was famine all over the world, people from nations around the world came to Egypt to buy grain from Joseph.

Lessons

1. Although Joseph asked Pharaoh's chief cup-bearer to plead on his behalf to the king to release him from prison because he had done nothing wrong to be imprisoned, he totally forgot about Joseph. However, at the right time or let's say in God's own appointed time, the events that

happened made the chief cup-bearer remember Joseph and his interpretation of their dreams. On this occasion, Pharaoh's chief cup-bearer did not even plead for Joseph's release from prison as Joseph requested, but rather he told Pharaoh that Joseph interpreted their dreams and his interpretations actually happened.

One of the lessons here is that do not despair when things do not happen at the time you expect them to happen, or you do not get your breakthrough at the time you have calculated. Things might not work out according to the sequence you wish them to, but the end result will be beautiful. You have to keep on working and also continue praying, trusting, and hoping that at the right time, in God's own appointed time, everything will work out for your good as it happened to Joseph. "He has made everything beautiful in his time." (Ecclesiastes 3:11a KJV). This reminds me of the song "In His Time He Makes All Things Beautiful" composed by Maranatha Singers:

Song – In His Time He Makes All Things Beautiful

> In his time, in his time
> He makes all things beautiful
> In his time

Lord please show me everyday
As you're teaching me your way
That you do just what you say
In your time

2. It is noteworthy the way and manner in which Joseph presented himself to King Pharaoh. He shaved himself and changed his clothes, which is befitting for how one should present oneself before an important person or dignitary like King Pharaoh. Obviously, the interpretation of Pharaoh's dreams changed Joseph's life. Yet, the decent manner in which he presented himself contributed, even if in a small way, to the perception Pharaoh had of Joseph. Perhaps this was a tradition when appearing before the king. But Joseph's turnout was appropriate, which built some trust.

3. Joseph acknowledged before Pharaoh that he is not the one who interprets the dreams but God, making him sound authentic. In other words, Joseph told Pharaoh that his ability to interpret dreams is a gift from God. Joseph gave the glory to God. So, when one is gifted or talented, it is right to acknowledge and give the glory to God.

4. After Joseph had interpreted Pharaoh's dreams, Pharaoh truly acknowledged that Joseph had a special gift and was filled with the spirit of God. Pharaoh, therefore, made Joseph ruler over Egypt, his house, and second in command to himself. Wow! What an honor that was given to God's humble servant Joseph. Yes indeed, "A man's gift makes room for him and brings him before the great" (Proverbs 18:16). So, it's important to know and use your gift. Everybody has a gift or talent.

5. The names Joseph gave to his sons were like a summary of his life's journey, from the time of being sold to his current state as the Prime Minister of Egypt. Their names were a way of thanking God and also an acknowledgment of God's goodness and faithfulness for seeing him through the very challenging and traumatic times into happiness and abundance. Joseph lost his family of origin when he was alone in Egypt, in a strange land as a teenager. However, God gave him a new family—his wife and children—and also Pharaoh and the people of Egypt.

Joseph named his firstborn son Manasseh. For he said, "God has made me forget all my hardship and all my father's house." (Genesis 41:51). Indeed, Joseph went through a lot: physical, psychological, and emotional abuse when his older brothers stripped him of his clothes and put him naked in a dry pit and then finally sold him to strangers. Remember, Joseph was a teenager, and that must have been very traumatic for him, not only because of the aforementioned evil actions of his brothers against him but also because they were his very own brothers whom he loved. That must have come as a complete shock to him. Joseph was also sexually abused by Potiphar's wife, but he did not yield to the pressure of sleeping with her. This is what landed Joseph in prison, something he did not consent to but was falsely accused of. Joseph came to Egypt with nothing, but God restored him and gave him more than he expected.

Joseph called his second son Ephraim, meaning "For God has made me fruitful in the land of my affliction" (Genesis 41:52). Who would have thought that Joseph would become the Prime Minister of Egypt? This is the very country in which he served as a slave and was also imprisoned for years. Yet, "the tide turned" for Joseph when he interpreted King Pharaoh's dreams, and he was made the Prime Minister of Egypt. Pharaoh gave Joseph a wife, and they had two boys, a family of his own! Joseph became very powerful, rich, and had a family of his own in Egypt. Joseph attributed all of these blessings to God and said that God had made him fruitful by every standard in the land of his affliction. "You have turned my mourning into dancing for me; you have taken off my sackcloth and clothed me with joy, that my soul may sing praise to you and not be silent. O Lord my God, I will give thanks to you forever" (Psalms 30:11-12 Amplified Bible).

6. Once again, Joseph's interpretation of dreams happened just as he told Pharaoh. There were seven years of plenty and abundance of food in Egypt, followed by seven years of severe famine after the abundance had ended. That was when Joseph opened all the storehouses and sold food to the Egyptians and people who came from all over the world to buy grain.

Chapter 5

Fulfillment

When Jacob heard that there was grain for sale in Egypt, he asked all ten of his sons, with the exception of Benjamin, to go to Egypt and buy grain for their family so that they would not die of hunger. Jacob did not allow Benjamin to go with his brothers to Egypt because he was afraid that something bad might happen to him. Therefore, the ten brothers left Canaan and went to Egypt to buy food, as their father had asked them to do.

Since Joseph was the Prime Minister of Egypt, he was the one responsible for selling grain to the Egyptians and all who came from other countries to buy food. Upon arrival in Egypt, Joseph's brothers came and bowed themselves before Joseph with their faces to the ground. When Joseph saw his brothers, he recognized them but treated them like strangers and spoke harshly to them. Joseph questioned his brothers, "Where do you come from?" and they responded, "From the land of Canaan, to buy food." (Genesis 42:7). Joseph recognized his brothers, but they did not recognize him. At this time, Joseph remembered the dreams he had dreamt of many years ago.

Joseph accused his brothers of being spies sent to spy on the land of Egypt, but they refused and said to him, "No, my lord, your servants have come to buy food. We are all sons of one man. We are honest men. Your servants have never been spies." (Genesis 42:10-11). Joseph insisted they were spies, but his brothers denied it and said, "We, your servants, are twelve brothers, the sons of one man in the land of Canaan, and behold, the youngest is this day with our father, and one is no more." (Genesis 42:13).

Joseph insisted that his brothers were spies and told them that he would keep nine of them in custody while one would be allowed to bring their youngest brother from Canaan to prove that they were honest men. Joseph then put all ten brothers in custody for three days as none of them left to bring their youngest brother. On the third day, Joseph told his brothers that he is a God-fearing man, and if they wanted to live, then they should prove their innocence by leaving one of their brothers in custody with him so that the rest would send food to their family in Canaan. They should bring their youngest brother on their return to Egypt for the release of their brother in custody. The brothers gave in to the pressure from Joseph, but before they embarked on their journey to Canaan, they had conversations among themselves that included their confession of what they did to their brother Joseph some years ago. They mentioned that the sin they committed against their brother had brought all of this evil upon them. Reuben answered them, "Did I not tell you not to sin against the boy? But you did not listen. So now there comes a reckoning for his blood." (Genesis 42:22). All the time Joseph used an interpreter, so they did not know that he understood them. On hearing this, Joseph turned away from them and wept. When Joseph returned, he spoke with them, took Simeon, and put him in custody right before their eyes. On Joseph's instructions, their bags were filled with grain, everyone's money was put back in his sack, and they were given provisions for their journey.

While on their journey back to Canaan, the brothers realized that their money had been put back in their sacks, and they trembled and said, "What is this that God has done to us?" (Genesis 42:28b). When the brothers arrived home in Canaan, they told Jacob their father everything that had transpired in Egypt and explained how they had to send their youngest brother to the lord of the land in Egypt to prove their innocence so that Simeon would be released from custody. Jacob and his sons were scared when they saw that all their money had been replaced in their sacks as they emptied them. Jacob was reluctant to send Benjamin, his youngest son, with his brothers to

Egypt because he thought he might not return and would lose him, in addition to Joseph and Simeon. Jacob said, "My son shall not go down with you, for his brother is dead, and he is the only one left. If harm happened to him on the journey that you are to make, you would bring down my grey hairs with sorrow to Sheol." (Genesis 42:38)

Lessons

1. Joseph was sold by his brothers when he was seventeen years old, a teenager. When his brothers went to buy grain in Egypt, Joseph was about forty years old. They did not recognize Joseph because over twenty years had now elapsed. Furthermore, they did not recognize him because never in their wildest dreams would they have imagined that after selling Joseph, he would become the Prime Minister of another country, Egypt. Who would have thought that a complete stranger would occupy such a powerful position in one of the most powerful nations in the world at the time? Well, it happened because, "with God, all things are possible" (Matthew 19:26b).

    Joseph's brothers bowed down to him when they came into contact with him as the Prime Minister of Egypt. That is exactly the dream that Joseph had back in Canaan as a teenager, which made his brothers very jealous of him and led them to sell him into slavery. Although Joseph's brothers got rid of Joseph by selling him into slavery to prevent his dreams from materializing, Joseph's dreams still happened because the dream came from God to save Jacob and his family and many people from dying of hunger during famine.

2. Joseph's brothers were confronted by their past. They initially lied to Joseph that one of their brothers had died, which was Joseph. However, when Joseph insisted that they were spies, they acknowledged their wickedness and confessed to each other in their language that their selling of Joseph many years ago had brought the evil of being accused as spies upon them.

3. Joseph was kind to his brothers despite the abominable thing they did by selling him to strangers. Joseph could have decided not to sell grain to them in the first place. However, he arranged for their sacks to be filled with grain and their money to be replaced in their sacks. According to Phil Waldrep in his book "Beyond Betrayal," Joseph did not trust his brothers because of how they betrayed him in the past and needed to work on trusting them again. That is why Joseph arranged for their money to be replaced in their sacks because he wanted to see if his brothers had changed from their old wicked ways and would return the money. This is to say

that after betrayal, if you choose to have a relationship with your betrayer, then you have to tread cautiously and rebuild trust slowly, little by little or one day at a time. It is your right to do so and not just resume a relationship with your betrayer as it was previously, only to be betrayed and hurt again.

4. Additionally, Joseph made provisions for everything that his brothers needed on their journey back to Canaan. Joseph could have retaliated and imprisoned his brothers, but he instead showed them kindness because he was a godly man. After all, God blessed Joseph and put him in that position of power so that he would be a blessing to his family and also to the nations. Joseph's actions set an example for us to be kind to those who have wronged us in their time of need. It takes a heart that has forgiven to be able to do that, and although it's a challenge, we can do it by asking for grace from God. It's also important to know that when you forgive others who have wronged you, you are doing it for your own good to do away with the toxicity that will hinder you from moving forward in life. It's healthier and a blessing for you to forgive.

Chapter 6

Tears of Joy

It is interesting to know that Jacob did not send Benjamin immediately with his brothers to meet Prime Minister Joseph in Egypt, until all the food they brought from Egypt had finished, and they needed more food to survive. The famine was still severe in Canaan and everywhere else, so Jacob asked his sons to go to Egypt and buy more grain. Judah replied that they could not go because the Prime Minister had said they could not see his face until they brought their brother with them. The argument went back and forth between Jacob and Judah until Jacob said his children had mistreated him by telling the Prime Minister that they had another brother in the first place. His sons replied, "The man questioned us carefully about ourselves and our kindred, saying, 'Is your father still alive? Do you have another brother?' What we told him was in answer to these questions. Could we in any way know that he would say, 'bring your brother down?'" (Genesis 43:7).

Judah told Jacob that if he did not allow them to go with Benjamin to Egypt to buy more food, the entire family, including their little ones, would die of hunger.

Judah added that he should be held responsible for Benjamin's safety and return to Jacob and that if anything bad happened to Benjamin, he should be blamed.

So Jacob agreed to allow his sons to go to Egypt with Benjamin to buy grain for the family. Jacob also told his sons to send some good-quality fruits, a little balm, a little honey, gum, myrrh, pistachio nuts, and almonds as a present to the Prime Minister.

Furthermore, Jacob told his sons to send double the money they would need in order to be able to return the money that they found in their sacks because it was probably an oversight. Jacob prayed for his sons' journey and said, "May God Almighty grant you mercy before the man, and may he send back your other brother and Benjamin. And as for me, if I am bereaved of my children, I am bereaved." (Genesis 43:14). So the brothers did exactly what their father told them, took the present and double the money, and Benjamin with them to see the Prime Minister of Egypt.

When Joseph saw Benjamin with his brothers, he instructed the manager of his house to bring them into his house and prepare lunch by killing an animal so they could dine with him. When the manager brought the brothers into Joseph's house, they were scared and thought that the Prime Minister was going to punish them because of the money that was put back in their sacks. They explained to the manager that someone had placed all the money they had used to purchase the grain the first time into their sacks, so they returned the money and brought additional funds to buy food. They also mentioned that they did not know who had put the money into their sacks. The manager reassured them, saying they should not be afraid because he had received their money, and it was their God and the God of their fathers who had placed the treasure in their sacks for them. Then the manager brought Simeon out to join his brothers.

When Joseph came home, his brothers presented the gifts they had brought from Canaan and bowed down to the ground before Joseph. Joseph inquired about their welfare and also asked if their elderly father was well and alive. When Joseph saw his brother Benjamin, his mother's son, he said, "Is this your youngest brother, of whom you spoke to me? God be gracious to you, my son!" (Genesis 43:29). Joseph was deeply moved by seeing his brother Benjamin and went to his bedroom to weep. Afterward, he washed his face and returned to them. At Joseph's command, food was served. Joseph dined alone, while his brothers were served at a separate table, with Benjamin receiving five times as much food as any of his brothers. They ate, drank, and rejoiced with

Joseph. The Egyptians who dined with Joseph were also served separately, as it was considered an abomination for Egyptians to eat with Hebrews.

Lessons

1. Although there was a famine in Canaan, like in other places around the world at the time, and Jacob and his sons did not fully understand what was happening between them and the Prime Minister of Egypt, Jacob sent a present with his sons to Prime Minister Joseph. The present was likely sent as a token of peace and, in doing so, to ease the ongoing tension. It also shows that Jacob was generous and could give even during the challenging time of famine.

2. Once again, Prime Minister Joseph was gracious to his brothers, who had mistreated him in the past because he had forgiven them. Joseph kept Simeon safe with him in Egypt and released him upon his brothers' arrival from Canaan. Furthermore, Joseph threw a festive lunch, or let's say a party, for his brothers when they returned to Egypt with Benjamin.

3. Joseph was ecstatic and emotional when he saw his little brother Benjamin because he had missed him very much, and also because he was alive and well. That's why he went into his bedroom to cry;

it was tears of joy. Joseph had also missed his father a lot, so he inquired of his brothers to know if their old father was alive and well, and they responded in the affirmative. Benjamin's presence showed Joseph that his brothers had not lied to him but were telling him the truth. Besides, Joseph's brothers brought back the money that had been put in their sacks. All of this indicated to Joseph that his brothers had changed from their old evil ways, and he was beginning to trust them again.

4. It is fascinating to know that even though it was an abomination for Egyptians to sit at a table and eat with Hebrews because, traditionally, every shepherd was considered an abomination to the Egyptians (Genesis 46:34), Joseph was made the Prime Minister of Egypt and second in command to Pharaoh, the King of Egypt. This is what I call the favor factor from God, due to his divine gift of interpreting dreams. The favor of God can open any door and bring you before kings.

Chapter 7

The Test

It was time again for Joseph's brothers to buy grain and return to Canaan. So the Prime Minister commanded the steward of his house to fill their sacks with food and put each man's money back in the mouth of the sack. Also, Joseph told the steward to put his silver cup in the sack of the youngest man in addition to the money. The steward did exactly as he was commanded.

Very early in the morning, the brothers set off on their journey to Canaan. Not long after they had left, Joseph asked his steward to intercept them on the way and say to them, "Why have you repaid evil for good? Is it not from this that my lord drinks, and by this that he practices divination? You have done evil in doing this." (Genesis 44:4-5).

When the steward intercepted the brothers and told them what Joseph had instructed him to say, they replied that they would never do such an evil thing and steal silver or gold belonging to the Prime Minister. They added that whoever is found to have taken the silver cup will die, and the rest of them will be servants to the Prime Minister. The steward agreed with the judgment that they had pronounced but with leniency and said that whoever they found to have stolen the silver cup would be his servant, and the rest of them would be free. The steward searched all of them and finally found the cup in Benjamin's sack to the amazement of all the brothers. After all, it was planned by Joseph and executed by his steward. They all returned to Egypt with the steward to Joseph's house. As soon as they saw the Prime Minister Joseph, they fell on the ground before him. Then Joseph, pretending, asked why they would even do something like that and think that he would not discover it. The brothers accepted that they had done wrong and willingly said they would be Joseph's servants, including Benjamin, in whose sack the silver cup was found. Joseph replied that he would never let all of them become his servants, but only the man in whose sack the cup was found would be his servant.

At this point, Judah approached the Prime Minister and pleaded with him to hear his story, asking him not to be angry because he knew he was as powerful as Pharaoh himself. Judah narrated the whole story of how their father had protested against their return to Egypt with Benjamin for several reasons. Firstly, Benjamin's older brother from the same mother had died, and he feared something bad would happen to

Benjamin if he traveled with them. Also, their father had only allowed them to travel with Benjamin because they had run out of food, and the Prime Minister had demanded that they should not see his face unless they came with their youngest brother to prove that what they told him about their family was true and that they were not spies. Furthermore, Judah said he had pledged to their father that he would ensure his youngest son, whom he loved, would return to him in Canaan. If harm should befall him, Judah should be held accountable and blamed for the rest of his life. Judah added that if Benjamin did not go back to his father, his father would die in sorrow. Therefore, Judah pleaded with the Prime Minister to allow Benjamin to return to his father, and he, Judah, would become the Prime Minister's servant and remain in Egypt to prevent his father from grieving to his death.

Joseph knew, as his brothers had told him, that it would be a terrible and sad situation for his brothers to return to their old father in Canaan without Benjamin, but he was pushing for that on purpose to reach a climactic point in the next chapter. Spoiler alert!

Lesson

Prime Minister Joseph obviously arranged for the money that his brothers used to purchase grain to be put back in their sacks because he did not want them to pay for the grain. Another important reason why Joseph instructed for the money to be put back in their sacks, including his silver cup in Benjamin's sack, was to engage his brothers in conversations to talk more about his family since he had been away from them for about twenty years when he was sold by his brothers to the Ishmaelite merchants.

Chapter 8

Forgiveness

When Judah pleaded with Joseph to allow Benjamin to return to his father and mentioned that Benjamin's older brother had died, Joseph became very emotional and couldn't control himself. He asked all those in his presence to leave, except for his brothers. He wept loudly, and the Egyptians, as well as Pharaoh's household, heard it. Then Joseph said to his brothers, "I am Joseph! Is my father still alive?" (Genesis 45:3). But his brothers couldn't respond because they were dumbfounded.

Joseph continued and said to his brothers, "I am your brother, Joseph, whom you sold into Egypt. And now do not be distressed or angry with yourselves because you sold me here, for God sent me before you to preserve life. For the famine has been in the land these two years, and there are yet five years in which there will be neither plowing nor harvest. And God sent me before you to preserve for you a remnant on earth, and to keep alive for you many survivors. So it was not you who sent me here, but God. He made me a father to Pharaoh and lord of all his house and ruler over all the land of Egypt. Hurry and go up to my father and say to him, 'Thus says your son Joseph, God has made me lord of all Egypt. Come down to me; do not tarry. You shall dwell in the land of Goshen, and you shall be near me, you and your children and your children's children, and your flocks, your herds, and all that you have. There I will provide for you, for there are yet five years of famine to come, so that you and your household, and all that you have, do not come to poverty. And now your eyes see and the eyes of my brother Benjamin see that it is my mouth that speaks to you. You must tell my father of all my honor in Egypt, and of all that you have seen. Hurry and bring my father down here." (Genesis 45:4-13). Then Joseph embraced his brother Benjamin, weeping in the process, while Benjamin also did the same. Joseph kissed all of his brothers and embraced them in tears. After the hugging and kissing, Joseph's brothers talked with him.

Pharaoh and his servants were glad to hear that Joseph's brothers had come to Egypt. Pharaoh asked Joseph to tell his brothers to go to Canaan and bring their father and families to come and live in Egypt. Pharaoh added that he would give the best part of the land of Egypt to Joseph's family when they moved to Egypt so that they could enjoy their lives there. Following Pharaoh's instructions, Joseph gave his brothers wagons and provisions for their journey back to Canaan. Joseph provided a change of clothes to each of his brothers, but to Benjamin, he gave five changes of clothes and three hundred shekels of silver. Joseph sent ten donkeys to his father loaded with the finest goods of Egypt and ten female donkeys loaded with grain, bread, and provisions for the journey. As Joseph's brothers were about to set off, he specifically told them not to quarrel on the way.

When Joseph's brothers arrived in Canaan, they told their father Jacob, "Joseph is still alive, and he is ruler over all the land of Egypt" (Genesis 45:26). Jacob's initial response to the news was utter disbelief and numbness of heart. However, when his sons gave him the message from Joseph and he saw the wagons with goods and food sent by Joseph, Jacob's spirit was revived. Then Jacob said, "It is enough; Joseph my son is still alive. I will go and see him before I die" (Genesis 45:28)

Lessons

1. When Joseph revealed himself to his brothers, the first question he asked them was if his father was alive. It shows that Joseph really loved his father and had missed him terribly after over twenty years of separation since he was sold by his brothers. Joseph's desire to see his father one day

might have been part of the dream that kept his hope alive.

2. Joseph's brothers were dumbfounded because they never, in their wildest dreams, expected Joseph to amount to anything good in life after selling him to the Ishmaelite traders, let alone become the Prime Minister of Egypt. This is a testament to the fact that when we trust in God, obey His word, and work hard, He causes the dreams that He gives us to materialize no matter the challenges or betrayals that one encounter.

3. Can you imagine? Joseph consoled his brothers not to be angry or distressed with themselves for selling him to the traders who further sold him into Egypt because he added, "God sent me before you to preserve life... to preserve for you a remnant on earth and to keep alive for you many survivors. So it was not you who sent me here, but God" (Genesis 45:5b-8a). Really? The ordinary person would have, in the nicest way, probably said, "Tada! I am still alive, and I am also the Prime Minister of Egypt. Your evil plot against me did not materialize. Did you see yourselves bowing before me?" and so on and so forth. However, Joseph was a godly man and therefore did the contrary, acknowledging the

goodness and faithfulness of God in his life, for his family and other people all over the world.

4. Everything Joseph did indicated that he had forgiven his brothers for the evil they did to him. Not only had he forgiven his brothers, but he was also generous to them. Joseph not only invited his father and innocent brother Benjamin to come and live with him in Egypt, but he also invited all his brothers to come along with their families for him to take care of them. In actual fact, Reuben was also innocent because he advised his brothers not to kill Joseph but to throw him into the empty pit. Reuben's plan was to rescue Joseph later and send him to his father, but his brothers sold Joseph in Reuben's absence and pretended they did not know his whereabouts.

5. Joseph had forgiven his brothers much earlier, after he was sold to the traders; that is why God gave him favor before Potiphar as well as the head guard of the prison. In both places, Joseph found favor and excelled in everything he did. Unforgiveness and bitterness in one's heart are hindrances to progress in life and true fellowship with God. It is a pure heart and genuine fellowship with God that opens the door for one to fulfill his or her destiny. Hence, the doors opened for Joseph to fulfill his destiny as he saw

in his dreams: the leader of his family, as he was destined to be. "Therefore, since we are surrounded by so great a cloud of witnesses, let us also lay aside every weight, and sin which clings so closely, and let us run with endurance the race that is set before us. Looking to Jesus, the founder and perfecter of our faith, who for the joy that was set before him endured the cross, despising the shame, and is seated at the right hand of the throne of God." (Hebrews 12:1-2).

Some Helpful Tips on Forgiveness

a. The Cambridge Dictionary defines forgiveness as "to stop blaming or being angry with someone for something that person has done or not punish them for something they have done."

b. Forgiveness is a decision to forgive one's offender, not necessarily because they deserve it or have asked for forgiveness, but because it helps you to get rid of ill feelings and resentment that can be consuming and detrimental to your health and overall well-being.

c. Research indicates that not forgiving those who have wronged you can significantly affect one's health in a number of ways, leading to heart disease, high blood pressure, depression, and anxiety, among others. On the contrary, forgiveness leads to better health and general well-being.

d. Forgiveness is a process and can take some time. However, the most important thing is to decide in your heart to start the journey of forgiveness and work towards it.

e. Forgiveness does not mean that you forget what your offender has done to you. As in the case of Joseph, from the time his brothers sold him to the time he encountered them again in Egypt was over twenty years, but Joseph had not forgotten what his brothers did to him. However, Joseph had forgiven his brothers.

f. Forgiving your offender does not automatically mean that you should have a relationship with them. It depends on your relationship with the offender and what they did to you. For example, if a family member offends you and you forgive them, they would continue to be a member of your family, but you can choose the kind of relationship you want to have with them going forward. You have to protect your heart and yourself from being hurt over and over again. You should not allow yourself to be mistreated and disrespected by your offender. That is why it is important to put some boundaries in place if they have to be in your life and consciously and slowly rebuild trust again.

g. As mentioned earlier in Chapter Five of this book, Joseph did not reveal himself to his brothers when he encountered them for the first time as the Prime Minister of Egypt. He asked that the money his brothers had used to buy grain be put back in their sacks because he wanted to find out if his brothers had changed from their old wicked ways and would return the money or not. And indeed, his brothers returned the money. When Joseph's brothers came for the second time to Egypt, Joseph asked them to leave their brother Benjamin with him after his silver cup, which Joseph had his steward plant in Benjamin's sack, had been found. Joseph wanted to see if his brothers would abandon Benjamin. These were all ways that Joseph used to find out if he could trust his brothers again before he revealed himself to them as Joseph, Joseph's brothers had to pass all of these tests before Joseph revealed himself to them as Joseph, their brother whom they had sold.

h. If you are the offender or betrayer, then you have to allow yourself to be held accountable for your wrongdoing if you want to have a relationship with the one you wronged or betrayed, whether it is a family member or friend. You should genuinely be sorry for wronging your friend, partner, family member, or colleague and ask for their forgiveness. You should also be patient for the one you wronged to slowly rebuild trust in you if you want a relationship with them again.

i. It is important to bear in mind that if you are a person of faith, then God requires that you forgive those who have wronged you, as He forgives you your sins in the Lord's prayer (Matthew 6:12). "For if you forgive others their trespasses, your heavenly Father will also forgive you, but if you do not forgive others their trespasses, neither will your Father forgive your trespasses" (Matthew 6:14-15).

Chapter 9

Reunion

The big day came when Jacob and his household, including his children, grandchildren, daughters-in-law, and all that they had, including their livestock, moved to Egypt on Joseph and Pharaoh's invitation. On their journey to Egypt, Jacob, being a God-fearing man, offered sacrifices to the God of his father Isaac at Beersheba. In the night, God spoke to Jacob in visions and assured him that he should not be afraid to go to Egypt because in Egypt, He would make Jacob, or Israel, into a great nation. God would go with him and would bring him out again, referring to the children of Jacob, and Joseph would bury him. Jacob did not make this life-transforming journey without a form of worship to God. The number of all the people in Jacob's household who came to Egypt was seventy.

Finally, Jacob and his household arrived in Egypt, and it was an emotionally charged and great reunion between Joseph and his father Jacob, to say the least. They cried, hugged, and kissed each other after a long separation of over two decades when Jacob thought that his son Joseph had been killed by a wild animal.

Joseph introduced his brothers to Pharaoh, and in obedience to what Joseph had told them, they pleaded with Pharaoh to live in the land of Goshen. Then Pharaoh replied and said to Joseph, "Your father and your brothers have come to you. The land of Egypt is before you; settle your father and your brothers in the best of the land. Let them settle in the land of Goshen, and if you know any able men among them, put them in charge of my livestock." (Genesis 47:5-6). So Pharaoh was very gracious and kind to Joseph's family when they moved from Canaan to live in Egypt during the famine. Then Joseph gave his father, his brothers, and their entire family a possession in the land of Egypt as Pharaoh had commanded. It was the best of the land, in Goshen, where they settled in order to be able to keep and shepherd their livestock. Moreover, Joseph provided food for his father, his brothers, and his father's entire household.

After living in Egypt for seventeen years, Jacob realized that his time to die was drawing closer. Therefore, he called his son Joseph and said to him, "If now I have found favor in your sight, put your hand under my thigh and promise to deal kindly and truly with me. Do not bury me in Egypt, but let me lie with my fathers. Carry me out of Egypt and bury me in their burying place." (Genesis 47:29-30). Joseph replied that he would honor his father's request, and Jacob made Joseph swear to him.

Lesson

It is astounding that Pharaoh and the Egyptians wholeheartedly welcomed Jacob and his household, who were shepherds, to live in Egypt, because customarily every shepherd was an abomination to the Egyptians (Genesis 46:34). This could only be attributed to the favor that God gave Joseph and his people before Pharaoh. "With man, this is impossible, but with God all things are possible" (Matthew 19:26).

Chapter 10

Final Words of Jacob

Not long after Jacob's conversation with Joseph about burying him with his fathers when he dies, Joseph received a report that his father was ill. Joseph, therefore, visited Jacob with his two sons, Manasseh and Ephraim. When they arrived, Jacob gathered some strength and sat up in his bed to have a conversation with his son. Because Jacob was very old, he could not see, so he inquired about Joseph's sons, asking who they were. Joseph responded that they were his sons whom God had given him in Egypt. Then Jacob asked Joseph to bring his sons closer for him to bless them, and he did. Jacob kissed Manasseh and Ephraim, embraced them, and said to Joseph, "I never expected to see your face, and behold, God has let me see your offspring also" (Genesis 48:11).

Jacob stretched forth his hands and laid them on Ephraim and Manasseh, blessing Joseph, saying, "The God before whom my fathers Abraham and Isaac walked, the God who has been my shepherd all my life long to this day, the angel who has redeemed me from all evil, bless the boys; and in them let my name be carried on, and the name of my fathers Abraham and Isaac; and let them grow into a multitude in the midst of the earth" (Genesis 48:15-16).

Jacob also blessed Manasseh and Ephraim, saying, "By you, Israel will pronounce blessings, saying, 'God make you as Ephraim and as Manasseh'" (Genesis 48:20).

After blessing them, Jacob told Joseph that he was about to die, but God would be with Joseph and send him back to the land of his fathers. Also, Jacob disclosed that he had given to Joseph a land property, a mountain slope that he took from the Amorites through war.

Subsequently, Jacob asked for all his sons to gather around him, and he spoke to each one of them his final words about their future. Also, Jacob told his sons that he was about to die, and when he died, they should bury him in the cave that is in the field at Machpelah, which is to the east of Mamre in the land of Canaan. Jacob added that this is the cave that Abraham bought as a burial place for his family, where Abraham and his wife Sarah, Isaac and his wife Rebecca, as well as Leah, Jacob's wife, were all buried.

When Jacob had finished talking to his sons, he went back to his bed, breathed for the last time, and died. Jacob died at the age of one hundred and forty-seven years.

Lesson

As is the norm, when Jacob knew he was about to die, he made all the necessary arrangements before passing on to be with his fathers. One of them was blessing his son Joseph and his children, and also all of his sons, according to their lives. Then he proceeded to tell his children the exact place to bury him, with his fathers and family. These words from Jacob were very important because they were his "dying wish." A dying wish is the final wish, request, or words made shortly before a person dies.

Chapter 11

Family Tree of Jacob

Abraham was Jacob's grandfather, and Sarah was Jacob's grandmother.

Isaac was Jacob's father, and Rebecca was Jacob's mother.

Esau was Jacob's twin brother.

Jacob married Leah ,and Rachel, and both of them died before Jacob. Leah had six sons and a daughter with Jacob, while Rachel had two sons with him. Rachel's servant Bilhah had two sons for Rachel with Jacob, and Leah's servant Zilpah also had two sons for Leah with Jacob. In total, Jacob had twelve sons and a daughter, as already mentioned in the first chapter of this book.

Author of Genogram: Oforiwah Penney-Laryea

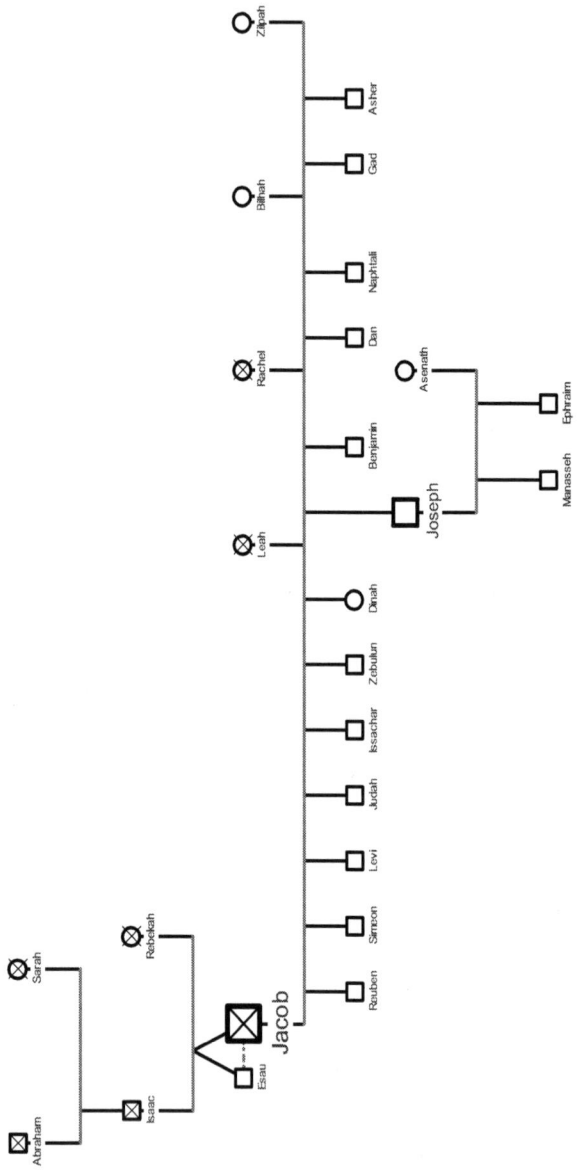

Chapter 12

God's Good Plans

Right after Jacob died, Joseph cried, embraced, and kissed his father for the last time. Then Joseph asked his physicians to embalm Jacob, which they did. The Egyptians mourned for Jacob for seventy days, and after that, Joseph asked permission from Pharaoh to go and bury his father in Canaan, as Jacob had instructed him and his siblings to do. Joseph received Pharaoh's full blessing to go and bury his father in Canaan. When he was leaving, Joseph was accompanied by all the servants of Pharaoh, the elders of his household, and all the elders of the land of Egypt, as well as the entire household of Joseph, his brothers, and his father's household. It was a very large group of people that went with Joseph and his family to bury Jacob in Canaan. The only people left behind in Goshen were their children. Furthermore, chariots and horsemen went with Joseph and the mourners to Canaan. After the burial of his father, Joseph returned to Egypt with his brothers and all the people who accompanied him.

After the death of their father, Joseph's brothers became afraid and thought that Joseph would repay them for all the evil they had done to him in the past. So they sent a message to Joseph, saying that before their father's death, he asked Joseph to please forgive his brothers for all the evil they had committed against him. On hearing this message, Joseph wept because it saddened his heart. Also, Joseph's brothers went and lay down before him, saying, "Behold, we are your servants" (Genesis 50:18). Then Joseph replied and said to them, "Do not fear, for am I in the place of God? As for you, you meant evil against me, but God meant it for good, to bring it about that many people should be kept alive, as they are today. So do not fear, I will provide for you and your little ones" (Genesis 50:19-21). That is how Joseph spoke kindly to his brothers and relieved them of their fears of retaliation from him.

Joseph kept his promise to his brothers and continued to be kind and provide for them until he died at the age of one hundred and ten years. Joseph was blessed and lived long enough to see his great-grandchildren before he died.

Lessons

1. Considering the support that Joseph and his family received from Pharaoh, his servants, the elders, and the people of Egypt when his father died, one could clearly see that Joseph was truly loved and cherished by Pharaoh and the people of

Egypt. It should be noted that Joseph was not an Egyptian by blood or birth. This can be seen as a special favor from God as a result of Joseph forgiving his brothers and all those who had wronged him in the past, and just availing himself to be his best in every situation and position he occupied with the help of God to fulfill his destiny.

2. It really saddened Joseph's heart when his brothers came to beg him for forgiveness again after the death of their father Jacob. This was because Joseph had moved past the evil his brothers did against him many years ago. Joseph also realized and told his brothers that they meant evil against him by selling him to the Ishmaelite traders, but God meant it for good to save the lives of many people in Egypt and around the world, including that of his family, during the seven years of famine.

Chapter 13

Life Is a Paradox

Life is a paradox because the very challenges that one encounters in life, which could easily cripple you, are the ones that, if you are able to endure and go through successfully, make you stronger and able to thrive in life. In many testimonies, like Joseph's story, it is the challenges that prepare you for your purpose, dream, and destiny in life.

In life, one is bound to go through challenges and offenses, and some of them could be very impactful and life-changing, like the betrayal of Joseph by his brothers. However, the way one handles these challenges will determine whether you get stuck in life or are able to move on and be successful in your future relationships and endeavors. Joseph chose forgiveness over bitterness and anger, which freed him to be his best as a slave in Potiphar's house, as a prisoner, and finally as the Prime Minister of Egypt. Also, there is a saying that "the bigger the dream, the bigger the challenges to achieve it." Therefore, do not allow the challenges of life, betrayal, and offenses to hold you back from achieving your dreams. When you forgive those who have betrayed and wronged you, you are doing the right thing and freeing your heart from revenge and darkness to achieve your purpose and dreams in life. Forgiving does not necessarily mean forgetting, as we saw in the case of Joseph and his brothers; rather, it is a conscious effort, a gift you give yourself to be open to greater possibilities and good.

Another important reason why forgiveness is necessary is because of the health benefits. A number of studies have revealed that not forgiving others can have adverse effects on one's health, leading to heart disease, insomnia, high blood pressure, and depression, among others. On the contrary, forgiveness leads to better health and an improved quality of life as a whole.

In the Lord's Prayer, it mentions that our Father God forgives us our sins even as we forgive those who sin against us (Luke 11:4). If you can't forgive and feel very bitter, you can pray for divine help and the grace to be able to forgive and/or seek professional help from a therapist or counselor, or someone you trust who is in a position to help you. If we are able to forgive one another, as Joseph did in this story, our families, communities, countries, and the world will be a better place to live.

The Bible Journey | Joseph is sold into slavery in Egypt

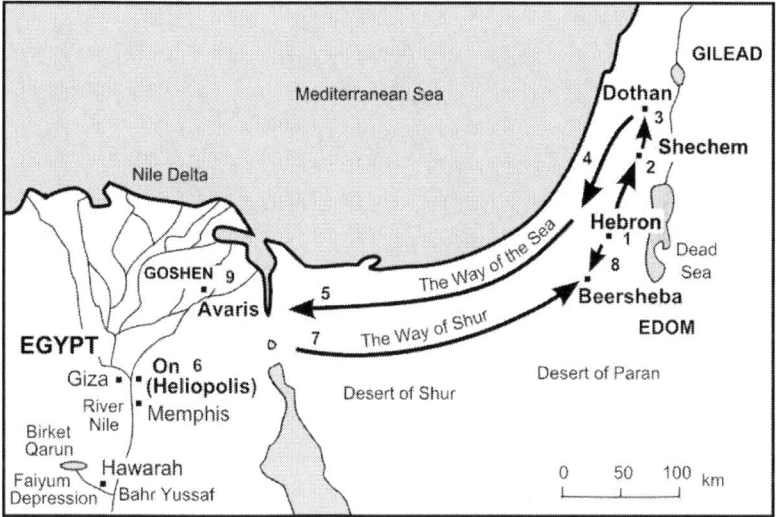

The Bible Journey | Joseph is sold into slavery in Egypt

References

1. GenoPro Beta.
   http://www.genopro.com/beta/

2. Johns Hopkins Medicine. (n.d.).
   Forgiveness: Your Health Depends on It.
   https://www.hopkinsmedicine.org/health
   /wellness-and-prevention/forgiveness-
   your-health-depends-on-it

3. Ryckman, S. (2022, February). *Sibling
   rivalry.* C. S. Mott Children's Hospital.
   https://www.mottchildren.org/posts/your
   -child/sibling-rivalry

4. Scarlet (2021, February 16). *How to deal with
   family betrayal.*
   Family Focus Blog.
   https://familyfocusblog.com/when-
   family-betrays-you/

5. The Bible Journey | Joseph is sold into slavery
   in Egypt.
   thebiblejourney.org/biblejourney2/24-the-

journeys-of-isaac-jacob-joseph/joseph-is-sold-into-slavery-in-egypt/

6. Waldrep, Phil. *Overcome Past Hurts + Begin To Trust Again – BEYOND BETRAYAL.* Narrated by Phil Waldrep, Audible, 2019. Audiobook.

"It's not what happens to you, but how you react to it that matters."

Epictetus

Like the story of Joseph in this book, life can be very challenging when one is betrayed by the people you love and trust. Joseph was not only betrayed by his brothers, who sold him into slavery, but was also framed by his master's wife, which landed him in prison. Despite all of these challenges, Joseph chose to stay positive.

If Joseph had chosen to be negative in life because of all of the above challenges and decided not to forgive his brothers, he would have remained stuck in his past and wouldn't have had the positive energy to propel him toward his dream. Forgiveness leads to better health and a better quality of life as a whole.

This book provides helpful information on forgiveness, how to deal with betrayal, and how to persevere in difficult times, among other topics. With tips on how parents can treat their children to minimize sibling rivalry, you will learn how to foster unity, friendship, and love in your family.

About The Author

Oforiwah Penney-Laryea, also known as Ofo, obtained her MS degree in Marriage and Family Therapy from Mercy College in New York, USA. She completed her practicum at St. Christopher's Inc. in Dobbs Ferry, where she worked with emotionally challenged teenagers and their families. Ofo is also a graduate of the University of Ghana-Legon, where she earned her bachelor's degree in Sociology with Psychology. As a Marriage and Family Therapist (MFT), Ofo has volunteered and worked with women in therapy and currently works with couples in premarital counseling and couples therapy, as well as with families. Ofo is a Christian and is married with three children.

Manufactured by Amazon.ca
Bolton, ON